THE
Cantor

IN THE LUTHERAN TRADITION

CARL SCHALK

CENTER *for*
CHURCH MUSIC

CONCORDIA PUBLISHING HOUSE · SAINT LOUIS

Dedicated to the memory of
Paul Bouman
August 26, 1918—April 28, 2019
whose life and work remain for many the model of
the Lutheran cantor

Published by Concordia Publishing House
3558 S. Jefferson Avenue
St. Louis, MO 63118-3968
1-800-325-3040 • cph.org

Published under the auspices of:
Center for Church Music
Concordia University Chicago
River Forest, IL 60305-1499

Manufactured in the United States of America

1 2 3 4 5 6 7 8 9 10   31 30 29 28 27 26 25 24 23 22

Contents

INTRODUCTION

The word *cantor* is the traditional term used by Lutherans for those responsible for "shaping, developing, and nurturing the musical life of the congregation at worship."[1] While a cantor's specific duties may vary from one congregation to another, they typically include leading the music of the congregation from the organ or a keyboard, preparing and directing a variety of choirs and instrumental ensembles, and planning and carrying out an effective music program in the life of the congregation.

The title of "cantor" suggests a larger sense of vocation, purpose, and ministry than many might associate with titles such as "director of music," "organist," or "choir director." It suggests a broader understanding and vision. It resonates to a greater sense of purpose.

The term "cantor" should not be reserved only for larger congregations with abundant musical resources. It is, in fact, in smaller congregations that the cantor can be particularly effective. But whatever the circumstances, the role of cantor in Lutheran congregations can be important and crucial in developing and nurturing a richer worship life.

While the term "cantor" reaches back long before the sixteenth-century Reformation, Lutherans continued its use. It was in the period between the first Lutheran cantor and friend of Martin Luther, Johann Walter (1496–1570),[2] and its most prominent cantor in the eighteenth-century, Johann Sebastian Bach

---

1   Carl Schalk, *A Small Catechism: Understanding Music in the Lutheran Tradition* (Minneapolis: Lutheran University Press, 2017), 19.

2   See Walter E. Krueger, "Walter, Johann," in *Lutheran Service Book: Companion to the Hymns* (St. Louis: Concordia Publishing House, 2019), 2:730–31.

(1685–1750), that the foundations of Lutheran music became clear, shaped by men such as Georg Rhau (1488–1548), Michael Praetorius (1571–1621), Samuel Scheidt (1587–1654), Johann Hermann Schein (1586–1630), Heinrich Schütz (1585–1672), and many others whose names we will never know. But today, as then, most Lutheran cantors carry out their duties little noticed as they faithfully work to nurture the musical tradition in the life of their congregation.

It is to those cantors, past and present, in whose footsteps we all walk, attempting faithfully to carry out our vocation, nurturing the tradition and moving it forward, that this little booklet is dedicated.

1
The Cantor's Role

Lutheran cantors understand their role from two distinct yet inevitably interconnected perspectives. They are, to be sure, church *musicians.* They are, simultaneously, *church* musicians. An effective cantor is always conscious of both perspectives.

Music is the medium through which the cantor works. Cantors need specific musical skills, which they continuously seek to develop and improve. Such growth may occur through private individual study, formal academic training, attendance at conferences and seminars, or in mentoring situations. The cantor, from this perspective, is concerned with continued, intentional, personal growth in musical skills in the service of the worship life of the congregation.

The second perspective, equally important but often overlooked, is that the cantor is simultaneously a *church* musician. It is the *Church's* song they teach, tend, nurture, and lead in congregational life. As leaders of the *Church's* song, cantors must be theologically informed and astute in their theological judgment. The cantor's responsibility involves a commitment to the faith of the Church, its liturgical life, and the implications of the Church's theology for the musical aspects of the congregation's worship life.

Cantors are always teachers who nurture the faith through music and the liturgy. Just as theological understandings affect musical decisions, so musical decisions often have theological implications. The cantor needs, therefore, to be continually growing into a wider and deeper understanding of the Scriptures and Christian theology, the liturgy, its music, and the liturgical life of the Church. It is then that cantors can be most effective as they lead their congregations to experience that "living voice of the Gospel"[1] through music and the Word.

---

[1] See Christopher Boyd Brown, *Singing the Gospel: Lutheran Hymns and the Success of the Reformation*, Harvard Historical Studies 148 (Cambridge, MA: Harvard University Press, 2005), 14.

2

The Cantor and the Church's Tradition

The Lutheran Church, in its liturgy and music, stands unambiguously in the tradition of the Western Catholic Church. Martin Luther and the Lutheran Confessions make this perfectly clear.

> It is not now nor ever has been our intention to abolish the liturgical service of God.[1]

> Our churches are falsely accused of abolishing the Mass. The Mass is held among us and celebrated with the highest reverence. Nearly all the usual ceremonies are also preserved.[2]

Luther received this liturgical and musical tradition as a good and gracious gift of God, celebrated and nurtured it in his time, corrected it where he understood it to be in error, and handed it on to the generations following. It is the primary role of Lutheran cantors today to do the same: to receive that tradition as a gracious gift of God, to nurture and celebrate it, to move it forward in our time, and then to hand it over to the following generation.[3]

The purpose and function of this tradition is that the Gospel may continue to be heard, faith be nourished, and the spiritual life of congregations be deepened, broadened, strengthened, and enriched. It is never a static heritage, a mere repristinating of the past. Firmly rooted in the history and practice of the whole Church, it always simultaneously looks to the future. Lutheranism's

---

1   *Order of Mass and Communion* (1523), in *Liturgy and Hymns*, ed. Ulrich S. Leupold, vol. 53 of *Luther's Works: American Edition* (Philadelphia: Fortress, 1965), 20.

2   Augsburg Confession XXIV 1.

3   The Latin verb *tradere* from which *tradition* is derived means "to deliver," "to hand over," "to entrust for safe-keeping."

embrace of this Church's tradition is a reflection of its understanding that it stands in continuity with the one, holy, catholic, and apostolic Church.

It is precisely this understanding that provided both the context and content for the rich musical developments in the two centuries following the Reformation. This period has often been referred to as the "golden age of Lutheran Church music." It was a developing tradition that continued to be shaped largely by the structures of the Mass, the Offices, the Church Year, and a developing body of congregational hymnody. These structures continue to shape the Lutheran tradition today and to inspire congregations, church musicians, and composers alike.

It is this liturgical and musical heritage that cantors today—as in Luther's day—have the privilege of nurturing. We care for and celebrate it precisely because it is centered in the proclamation of the Gospel of Jesus Christ through Word and Sacrament. We do not celebrate it as a historical artifact. Rather, it is the high honor and holy calling of cantors to celebrate this gift as the living, vital reality it can continue to be in the worship life of the congregations they serve.

3

The Cantor and the Congregation's Song

The cantor's fundamental musical responsibility to the congregation is twofold:

1. To encourage, nurture, and support *the congregation's singing of the liturgy*

2. To encourage, nurture, and support *the congregation's use of a basic core of liturgical hymnody*

These two closely related responsibilities[1] are basic to the cantor's task, whether the congregation is small or large, whether the musical resources are modest or plentiful. While the suggestions that follow are applicable to all congregations, they can be particularly helpful in small congregations, even where there is no choir.

The first responsibility of the cantor is to help the congregation sing the liturgy with confidence and an ever-greater understanding.[2] In their role as teacher, cantors will offer regular opportunities to study the liturgy—its structure and movement, as well as its music. This may occur through adult education sessions, Bible classes, and the like. The cantor also teaches the congregation how the liturgy is best sung through appropriate modeling from the keyboard. As the congregation grows in its familiarity

---

1   It is important to note that the musical vehicle Luther chose to encourage the congregation's singing of the liturgy was the *chorale*, particularly those chorales that were paraphrases of the five great prose songs of the ordinary. These were the Kyrie—"Kyrie! God, Father" (*LSB* 942); the Gloria in Excelsis—"All Glory Be to God on High" (*LSB* 947, 948); the Creed—"We All Believe in One True God" (*LSB* 953, 954); the Sanctus—"Isaiah, Mighty Seer in Days of Old" (*LSB* 960); and the Agnus Dei—"O Christ, Thou Lamb of God" (*LSB* p. 198).

2   Through-composed musical settings of the liturgy for the congregation were first introduced in North American Lutheranism in the early twentieth century. Such settings by individual composers began to appear in the latter half of the twentieth century.

with and understanding of the liturgy, together with its regular participation in its celebration, the richness of the liturgical tradition and its meaning for the life of the congregation will continue to grow and deepen.[3]

The second basic responsibility of the cantor in relation to the congregation is to develop and nurture a basic repertoire of liturgically useful congregational hymnody. This is always a long-term activity that requires serious and persistent attention. Many hymns that belong in such a basic congregational repertoire—drawn from the historic treasury of the Church's song—may already be familiar in many congregations.[4] A convenient checklist of such hymns—and a place to begin—are the lists of the Hymn of the Day, the chief hymn of every Sunday celebration and, in Lutheran circles, essentially a liturgical Proper.[5]

If hymns new to the congregation are to be successfully introduced, it is imperative that there is careful, thoughtful preparation, introduction, and follow-through as the new hymn gradually becomes part of the congregation's basic repertoire.

The following specific suggestions may be helpful in pursuing these two goals:

- Ask a small group from the congregation to serve as a central core of singers to support the congregational singing.
- Hold a one- or two-part adult education session for new (and old) members on "Learning to Sing the Liturgy."

---

3   Most congregations are well-served if they know and can sing with confidence two settings of the Divine Service. One setting may serve as the congregation's basic setting. A second might be used for more reflective or meditative seasons such as Advent or Lent.

4   A useful exercise would be to list the hymns sung in worship throughout the past year or two and how many times they were sung. Consider whether any have been sung too frequently. What hymns that the congregation does not yet know could be added to this list?

5   See *Lutheran Service Book: Hymn Selection Guide* (St. Louis: The Lutheran Church—Missouri Synod, 2006) and D. Richard Stuckwisch, "The Hymn of the Day," in *Lutheran Service Book: Companion to the Hymns* (St. Louis: Concordia Publishing House, 2019), 2:137–42.

- Write a column "From the Cantor" for the congregation's newsletter to teach and inform the congregation.

- Teach an adult education session on "The Shape of the Liturgy" to help explain why Lutherans worship as they do.

- Organize an occasional informal "hymn sing" with brief commentary on each hymn.

- Encourage every committee meeting during a particular liturgical season to begin or end by singing a hymn you would like the congregation to learn.

The cantor is always a teacher, helping the congregation—in a variety of ways beyond the regular liturgical celebrations—to a deeper and richer understanding and experience of worship.

4

The Cantor as Organist

The organ has played a significant role in Lutheran worship since the Reformation, though its initial role was quite different in the sixteenth century.[1] At that time, the chorales were sung in unison without accompaniment, as had been the case with the medieval chants upon which many of the chorales were based. It was not until the early seventeenth century that the organ began to assume the role of accompanying congregational singing and gradually established the pride of place it occupies today.

The organist in the Lutheran tradition is, by definition, a *liturgical* organist. The participation of the organist is determined by the specific requirements of the liturgical action. Carl Halter's words speak directly to this point.

> The way the organist functions in the service is determined by the movement and requirements of the liturgical action. It is the function of the liturgical organist to lead the congregation in the singing of the hymns and chorales, to accompany, as appropriate, other portions of the liturgy sung by the congregation or choir, and to present other liturgical or attendant music, alone or in an ensemble.[2]

---

1   For more information, see Herbert Gotsch, "The Organ in the Lutheran Service of the Sixteenth Century," *Church Music* 67, no. 1 (1967): 7–12; and Steven Wente, "The Organ in the Early Lutheran Reformation," in Daniel Zager and Steven Wente, *The Choir and the Organ in Early Lutheranism* (Minneapolis: Lutheran University Press, 2018).

2   See Carl Halter, "The Music of the Organ," in *Handbook of Church Music*, ed. Carl Halter and Carl Schalk (St. Louis: Concordia Publishing House, 1978), 23.

Moreover, Halter continues, "it is not the function of the organist to entertain, to provide meaningless meanderings at the keyboard, or to fill every quiet moment with music."[3]

Of all the skills the cantor needs, the ability to function well at the keyboard is the most obvious. To lead a congregation in singing the liturgy and hymns and to accompany a choir—and to do so with consistency, sensitivity, and flexibility—should be the primary goal of every church organist. This is a unique and distinct skill, a skill quite different from the ability to play organ literature.

The organist may also play preludes, postludes, and voluntaries during the gathering of the gifts. The organist usually introduces hymns and chorales with appropriate intonations or introductions that announce the tune and the general pace of the singing. The organist may on occasion use varied harmonization on specific stanzas of a hymn or—for organists so skilled—improvise a carefully thought-out hymn introduction. All these are skills liturgical organists are continually seeking to develop and improve according to their ability.

The organist is, in reality, the one who leads the congregation in its song. It is the organist who controls the pace of the singing as well as the character of the singing through the thoughtful choice of registration. The successful liturgical organist requires, to be sure, musical skills. But successful liturgical organists also require a sensitivity to the texts—whether hymns or liturgical—that they accompany.

The nature of the organ, its legato, sustaining quality, is such that, when played appropriately, it models for the congregation the way to sing. That is why the organ continues to be a very effective instrument to lead and accompany the congregation's song.

---

3   Halter, "Music of the Organ," 23.

5

The Cantor and the Choir

The choir in the Lutheran tradition is, by definition, a *liturgical* choir. The choir is part of the congregation yet simultaneously a distinct group, singing both with and on behalf of the congregation according to the specific liturgical action. The choir also provides a reliable core of singers to lead and support the congregation. Its presence is a visible and audible sign of stability and continuity.

Choirs come in different sizes, from small to large. There may be a women's choir, a mixed choir, a men's choir, a children's choir, or the one-person choir (solo voice). But whatever its size or makeup, the choir's purpose and function remain the same.

Two elements in particular in the liturgy normally call for the joint contribution of *congregation and choir together*:

- The singing of the Psalmody
- The singing of the Hymn of the Day

The Psalmody

The Psalmody is a basic element in both the Divine Service and in the Daily Offices (Matins and Vespers, Morning and Evening Prayer). In the Divine Service, the appointed Psalm is sung following the Old Testament Reading, usually with congregation and choir alternating, most commonly verse by verse. The psalms are usually sung to one of several formulary tones (*LSB*, p. xxvi). The singing of the appointed Psalm is normally preceded and followed by an antiphon sung by the choir or a solo voice. The pattern is as follows:

Antiphon (choir)

The appointed Psalm
    (alternating between choir and congregation)
Antiphon (choir)

The antiphon may be a newly composed setting or may be the same tone as the psalm, sung by a solo voice or the choir. The choir sings verse 1, modeling for the congregation the pace and manner of singing, followed by verse 2 sung by the congregation, and so on. Care should be taken that both antiphon and the formulary tone used for the psalm text are compatible. Occasionally, composed settings of the appointed psalm text or psalm paraphrases may be substituted.

When first introducing the singing of the Psalms by the congregation where it has not been the practice, it may be desirable to have the choir sing them alone for a period of time so that the congregation hears how they should be sung.

Singing the appointed Psalm each week by the congregation and choir is an important part of the choir's role. It requires careful preparation, diligent rehearsal, and persistent use until the practice becomes second nature for the congregation.

The Hymn of the Day

The congregation also participates with the choir in singing the Hymn of the Day (*de tempore* hymn) in alternation between these two groups (*alternatim praxis*).[1]

This practice gives choirs at every level of ability the opportunity to participate, from unison singing to part-settings of the hymn. Singing the complete hymn in this way gives the congregation a unique opportunity to meditate on its text. The following are two simple examples, among many possibilities, of such alternating singing.

---

1   For a variety of ways of alternating in this historic Lutheran practice, see Carl Schalk, *The Hymn of the Day and Its Use in Lutheran Worship* (St. Louis: Concordia Publishing House, 1983).

Organ Introduction		Organ Introduction	
Stanza 1	Congregation	Stanza 1	All Women
Stanza 2	Choir	Stanza 2	Choir
Stanza 3	Congregation	Stanza 3	All Men
Stanza 4	Choir	Stanza 4	Choir
Stanza 5	Congregation	Stanza 5	All

Other ways of alternating will readily suggest themselves.[2]

Choral settings of the Hymn of the Day are widely available. They can range from unison singing with or without accompaniment to part-settings, especially those settings written by a variety of composers for this purpose. Many composers, including Johann Sebastian Bach, have provided such choral settings. Two examples are show here to illustrate the range of possibilities. The first is a simple two-part setting of the Hymn of the Day for Advent 1; the second, a four-part setting of Melchior Vulpius.

2 See also Schalk, *Hymn of the Day and Its Use in Lutheran Worship.*

Two final categories of choral music are part of the choir's responsibility:

- The parts of the liturgy usually assigned to the choir because their texts change each week: the Gospel Acclamations and the Offertory
- The large group of Psalm, Gospel, and biblical motets, anthems, liturgical Passion settings for Holy Week, and the like

The Gospel Acclamations and Offertory

Two parts of the liturgy with Proper texts, which change each week and are therefore usually sung by the choir alone, are the Gospel Acclamations (Verse) and the Offertory. The Gospel Acclamations are sung both before and after the reading of the Gospel. If there is a Gospel Procession, the Acclamations may be sung during the Procession. The Offertory, also a Proper text, is sung as the gifts are brought forward for the celebration of Holy Communion. Because the gifts usually include the bread and wine, these Offertory texts frequently refer to the celebration of Holy Communion.

Other Attendant Music

Here are some examples of music for choir alone:

Biblical motets	Anthems
Psalm motets	Liturgical Passion settings
Gospel motets	Communion motets

Care must be taken when choosing music for the choir so that it not only is appropriate for the specific Sunday, feast, or festival but also is within the ability of the choir to sing with confidence. As to the place of these choral selections, unless they are associated with a particular part of the liturgy—as, for example, a Gospel motet or a Psalm motet—the traditional place is during the distribution of Holy Communion.

All choral music, even the simplest piece, takes time and effort to learn well. The cantor should begin teaching a new piece of music well before its intended use. Music should be selected that will find a lasting place in the choir's repertoire. Its repeated use, as appropriate, will make it part of the choir's DNA. For example, every choir should learn Heinrich Isaac's simple yet exquisitely beautiful four-part setting associated with the text "Now rest beneath night's shadow."[3] Use the stanza "Lord Jesus, who dost love me" as a closing prayer for choir rehearsals. It will soon become a significant part of each singer's musical and spiritual life.

Whether leading the music of congregation, choir, or both together, the cantor should always have in mind questions such as the following in the process of selecting music. These questions address basic theological, liturgical, musical, and practical considerations.

- Does the text reflect the faith of the Church?
- Is the music suitable for the liturgical season, Sunday, feast, or festival?
- Is the character of the music appropriate for its liturgical use?
- Is the length of the music suited for the liturgical action?
- Is the music within the choir's ability?
- Does a particular piece rise to the level that it might become a permanent part of the choir's repertoire?

Questions such as these should always be uppermost in mind in the planning and selecting of music for the choir.

---

3   Among numerous options, see the one included in Carl F. Schalk, *The Praetorius Chorale Book* (St. Louis: Concordia Publishing House, 2014).

6

The Cantor as Composer

Not every cantor will feel the necessity or have an interest in writing music for the Church. To write music for the public worship of God's people is a daunting task. Often the fledgling cantor/composer begins out of necessity—writing a simple descant for the choir, a short organ intonation, or a varied hymn accompaniment.

But whatever the immediate impulse to write even the simplest music for worship, two things are necessary. First is a basic grounding in the elements of the craft of music: music theory, musical form, counterpoint, the ability to craft a good melody, and so on. Music is many things, but at its base it is a craft, and the church musician as composer must have the basic elements of that craft well in hand. Second, the composer must have or develop the ability for merciless self-criticism. This is perhaps the most difficult attitude to develop, but it is crucial to the composer's task.

Composers for the Church work within the same parameters that shape all aspects of the cantor's task: the Church Year, the Psalmody for the day, the appointed lessons from Scripture, and the great treasury of the Church's hymnody. Here are some of these liturgical elements that offer opportunity for the composer:

Congregational hymn tunes

Hymn descants

Psalm antiphons

Offertory sentences

Gospel acclamations

Organ hymn intonations

Choral settings of the Hymn of the Day

Chorale concertatos

Biblical motets

Anthems

Gospel motets

To be truly successful as a composer for the Church, the cantor must be thoroughly acquainted with the context and parameters described earlier in this monograph. When in doubt, the liturgical composer is best served with reminders such as "Complex is not better than simple" and "Because you can doesn't mean you should." To aspire to write music for the public worship of the Church is certainly a high and noble calling. It is also a calling not to be undertaken lightly, but with humility, modesty, perseverance, and reverence.

7

The Cantor's Role: One More Perspective

At the beginning of this little treatise, two aspects of the cantor's role were mentioned: that of church *musician* and *church* musician. There is a third aspect of the cantor's role, however, that should permeate all that has been discussed here. Simply put, cantors truly *care* for those they teach, lead, and work together as they sing the Church's song.

Like the Good Shepherd, cantors know those in their care. They are truly concerned about them, not simply as parts of a music program but also as individuals who, like themselves, are on a journey of faith. They rejoice with them in times of accomplishment and celebration. They mourn with them in times of sorrow.

What unites the cantor and those they lead is the faith they share and the desire to give it expression through the gift of music. To be a member of a congregation or a choir whose cantor shares a common faith and purpose, to praise God through His gift of music, is a precious gift. To be a cantor serving such a congregation, open to explore the riches of the Lutheran tradition of worship and music, is a gift not to be underestimated.

To begin to move in the direction laid out in this little treatise will necessitate—in many congregations—a reexamination and reorientation of priorities and expectations of those involved in the Church's worship: musicians, pastors, and congregations alike. Many congregations are already on the way. For others it is a journey yet to begin.

For Further Reading and Viewing

ARTICLES

Fothergill, Chad, and Daniel Schwandt. "Re-Membering the Cantor's Vocation." *CrossAccent* 25, no. 3 (Fall/Winter 2017): 6–26.

Herl, Joseph, Peter C. Reske, and Jon D. Vieker, eds. *Lutheran Service Book: Companion to the Hymns.* Volume 2. St. Louis: Concordia Publishing House, 2019.

See especially Carl F. Schalk, "The Church's Song: Proclamation, Pedagogy, and Praise," 123–29; Richard Resch, "Hymns as Sung Confession," 131–36; and D. Richard Stuckwisch, "The Hymn of the Day," 137–42.

Nuechterlein, Herbert. "Cantorei." Pages 75–78 in *Key Words in Church Music.* Revised edition. Edited by Carl Schalk. St. Louis: Concordia Publishing House, 1978, 2004.

BOOKLETS

Bichsel, M. Alfred. *The Cantor in Historical Perspective.* ALCM Pamphlet Series. Fenton, MO: MorningStar, 1989.

This was a plenary presentation at the first biennial conference of the Association of Lutheran Church Musicians in 1987.

Leaver, Robin A. *The Theological Character of Music in Worship.* St. Louis: Concordia Publishing House, 1985.

Schalk, Carl. *A Small Catechism: Understanding Church Music in the Lutheran Tradition.* Minneapolis: Lutheran University Press, 2017. Published under the auspices of the Center for Church Music.

———, and Paul Westermeyer. *A Large Catechism: Understanding Church Music in the Lutheran Tradition.* Minneapolis: Lutheran University Press, 2017. Published under the auspices of the Center for Church Music.

———. *The Pastor and the Church Musician: Thoughts on Aspects of a Common Ministry.* St. Louis: Concordia Publishing House, 1984.

Various. *Living Voice of the Gospel: Dimensions in Wholeness for the Church Musician.* St. Louis: Concordia Publishing House, 1996.

BOOKS

Brown, Christopher Boyd. *Singing the Gospel: Lutheran Hymns and the Success of the Reformation.* Harvard Historical Studies 148. Cambridge, MA: Harvard University Press, 2005.

Fothergill, Chad. *Sing with All the People of God: A Handbook for Church Musicians*. Minneapolis: Augsburg Fortress, 2020.

Riedel, Johannes, ed. *Cantors at the Crossroads: Essays on Church Music in Honor of Walter E. Buszin*. St. Louis: Concordia Publishing House, 1967.

Schalk, Carl. *Johann Walter: First Cantor of the Lutheran Church*. St. Louis: Concordia Publishing House, 1992.

———. *Music in Early Lutheranism: Shaping the Tradition (1524–1672)*. St. Louis: Concordia Publishing House, 1999.

Westermeyer, Paul. *A High and Holy Calling: Essays of Encouragement for the Church and Its Musicians*. Fenton, MO: MorningStar, 2018.

———. *The Church Musician*. Minneapolis: Augsburg Fortress, 1997.

VIDEO

Fothergill, Chad. "The Lutheran Cantor in the Twenty-First Century." Center for Church Music, https://www.cuchicago.edu/academics /centers-of-excellence/center-for-church-music/conversations/.